Tuning your dinghy

Tuning your dinghy
Lawrie Smith

photographs by Tim Hore

Fernhurst Books

First published 1985 by
Fernhurst Books, 13 Fernhurst Road, London SW6 7JN

ISBN 0 906754 18 6

Acknowledgements

Thanks are due to Andy Barker and Mark Simpson who crewed for the photographic sessions in Weymouth Bay; to Michael Hicks for his detailed advice on the manuscript; and to Joan Buxton for typing it.

The publishers also gratefully acknowledge the permission of Roger Lean-Vercoe to reproduce the photographs on the following pages: 4 & 5, 7, 43, 45, 47, 49.

The cover photograph is by Kos, and the cover design by Behram Kapadia.

Composition by A & G Phototypesetters, Knaphill, Surrey
Printed by Ebenezer Baylis & Son Ltd, Worcester

Contents

1 Assembling the gear

Before embarking on any race programme you must decide the level of success you realistically hope to achieve, whether it be at club, national or international level. Your main restrictions will be natural ability, time and finance. If you have an abundance of all three then there is no reason why you cannot set your sights on winning a world title.

In this book I am assuming that you are already at a reasonable level of competence, and will try to help you get more speed out of your existing or new boat.

How to begin in a new class

First, do not choose to sail a boat that is unsuited to either your physical size or physical ability. For

instance, if you weigh 140 lb you will never succeed in a Finn dinghy but would have every chance in a 470. Therefore research carefully the optimum weight required for the class of boat you wish to sail. Similarly, if you feel you are very good at making a boat go fast but not so good tactically, then you would be more suited to a Flying Dutchman rather than, say, a Soling.

Once you have decided on a class you must then figure out what make of boat you should buy, and if it is then better to buy new or second-hand. As an example, you would be well advised to buy a proven second-hand FD with plenty of life left in it so that you can learn immediately how to sail the boat before worrying about the various complicated layout designs. If, however, you were buying a 470 you would do better to buy new, as 470s have a short optimum life.

Whatever boat you eventually buy it must be capable of achieving the same speed as the best in that class, so that you have no worries about other people who you suspect are going faster due to superior equipment. You will need a 'state of the art' hull that is the correct shape, down to minimum weight with perfect hull and foil finish. It will also need the same mast as the top boats, the same sails and other equipment.

It is essential when trying to get to the top to use proven equipment; only when you are on level terms with the best can you afford to experiment with your own ideas.

If you can't fathom out what is the best equipment, because the top people all seem to have different ideas, then spend time talking to them and find out why they use what they do. Many top sailors now use their own products and have no other choice, so you must find these things out and make your decision.

Left: The author tuning his 470. Opposite: the Flying Dutchman class is one of the most complicated dinghies to tune correctly.

Once you have chosen a sailmaker, explain your plans to him and ask him what he can do to help you. He should be able to give you measurements of spreader lengths and angles, mast rakes and shroud tensions of boats that are currently successful with his sails. If he says he can't, then ask him to find them out for you. He must also be able to repeat your sails should you wish to order another set prior to your championships. It will be no good spending months tuning your boat around your sails and achieving good speed, only to find that your sails have stretched out of shape and you can't repeat them in new material. Your sailmaker must, therefore, have a system of making sails from a pattern or template and must also have a system of testing the sailcloth because the cloth is just as important as the cut of the sail.

Too many times you find sailmakers changing their ideas and not being able to go back to previous designs as they've either lost their cut sheets or that particular batch of cloth is no longer available. All these things must be assessed or you could end up wasting your time and money.

2 Tuning on land

Before you set about tuning your boat, make sure what you are about to tune isn't going to break once you've finally got it right. For instance, don't waste time setting up a mast if it has small cracks and looks like it might break: buy a new one. Check your centreboard and rudder for defects, because if they break you will have to start all over again, having tuned your boat around them. Remember that each and every piece of equipment is working together, and if one is changed the others won't perform in the same way.

Make sure that all your control systems are as simple and efficient as possible. There is no excuse for a badly fitted-out boat, and before you even sail it you must have everything working perfectly.

Mast

Lay the mast along a bench and make sure the heel tenon is dead central and a perfect fit. If the tenon can move the mast will twist and your spreader settings will become haphazard. Working up the mast, check the gooseneck is central and is in the correct position relative to the black band. Check the spreader bracket is strong and will not deflect even 1 mm under load — if it does your spreader settings will be useless. Make sure the bracket is central by measuring from each edge to the luff groove in the mast.

Moving up the mast, check that the shrouds connect into the mast at their correct position according to class rules — in most classes this will be as high as possible. The trapeze wires should then be positioned slightly aft of the shrouds and 3 to 4 inches (75-100 mm) above, if allowed. Don't move them higher than this or you will create problems by inducing an S-bend in the mast.

The spinnaker halyard should be as high as the class rules permit. At the tip of the mast the black band must be as high as possible, leaving the least amount of metal above it; check then that the halyard will hoist the mainsail right up so that the top of the sail is level with the lower edge of the band. Any section of the spar above this point is unnecessary weight and windage just where it hurts performance most.

Before stepping the mast, set your boat up with a spirit level — making sure it is absolutely level, both sideways and fore and aft. Run a light string line from the centre of the bow to the centre of the stern. Using a plumb line, check that the mast step and mast gate are lined up and central in the boat. Then measure out to the gunwales, checking that the shroud plates are an equal distance from the centre and level with each other.

Below: Make sure the heel tenon is central and a tight fit in both the mast and the mast step.

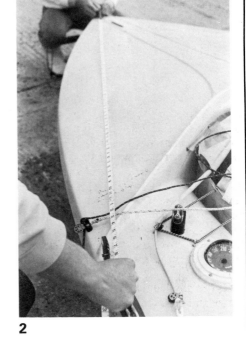

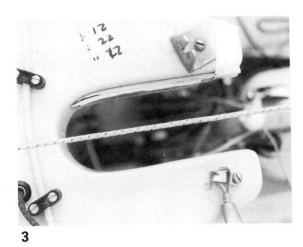

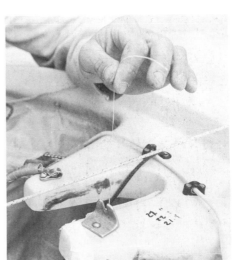

IS THE RIG CENTRAL?

Run a string from the bow to the centre of the stern.
1,2 Check the shroud plates are symmetrical.
3 If necessary, pad the mast gate to make it central.
4 Use a plumb line to ensure the step is vertically below the gate.

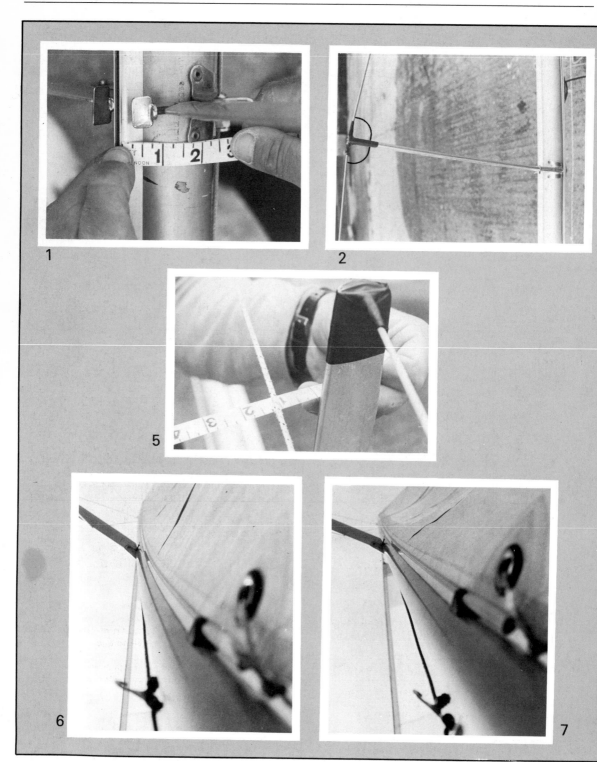

3

4

8

SETTING UP THE SPREADERS

1 Measure from each edge of the spreader bracket to the luff groove to ensure the bracket is central.

2 Arrange the spreaders in the vertical plane so they bisect the line of the shrouds.

3 You must be able to adjust the spreaders fore and aft; on this 470 spreader, screw adjusters do the trick.

4 On this 505 the spreader deflection is adjusted by moving the base of the shroud. Sliding the car forwards increases bend; sliding it aft decreases bend.

5 Now measure the fore and aft spreader angle as described on page 12 (the bow is on the left).

6,7 The spreaders are 1 inch (25 mm) further aft in (6). Note the larger prebend compared with (7), for light winds.

8 The crew is using screw adjusters to alter fore-and-aft spreader angle while afloat (with the jib halyard slackened off).

Spreaders

To set the spreaders accurately you will firstly need turn screw adjusters. If they are not allowed by class rules or you don't wish to use them, they are still the only way of setting the two spreaders the same; they can be removed once the spreaders have been marked and drilled.

Find out the average length of spreader the top boats are using and also the favoured bracket height, as the two are obviously related. If you have no idea of length or height, measure the distance between bracket and shroud with the mast stepped and shrouds connected and add four inches (100 mm) for a starting point.

Cut one spreader to length, lay it over the other and mark it off; finally check both are the same. Once you are happy, fit one side into the bracket, drilling through the outboard bolt hole of the bracket itself. Lay this spreader over the other and drill through it, making sure both holes line up before bolting them onto the bracket. Dress both shrouds down the mast under tension making sure they are both the same length. You can then step the mast into the boat next to a building or steps, enabling you to reach the spreaders when the mast is in the boat.

Connect the shrouds into the ends of the spreaders and fasten the shrouds into their plates. Take up tension on the rig and then adjust the height of each spreader so that the vertical angle it makes with the shroud is the same above and below (see photo on page 10). You must then fasten each shroud to its spreader using seizing wire; it is essential that the shroud cannot slide through the spreader end. If it does you will either increase or decrease the sideways pressure on the mast.

You now have a mast with spreaders equal both in length and vertical angle. All that is left is to determine fore and aft angle.

- Firstly, make sure both spreaders are raked back equally. Set up a string line from the top of the shroud (fastening it with tape) and stretch it taut down to the shroud plates at deck level. Set both adjusters so that each spreader just touches the string.
- Next, see the spreaders in a sensible starting position. Turn both adjusters equally until the spreaders are angled about 1 inch (25 mm) forward of the string line. This is a good

starting position — fine tuning will come later.
- Finally, measure and record the amount of spreader rake.

Count the number of threads on each adjuster so you can find the position again when you're afloat. For a more accurate record, measure the distance between a straight line formed by the two tips and the aft face of the mast. This then gives you a precise base to work from. For example my 470 spreaders are 18½ inches (470 mm) long and swept back 5½ inches (140 mm) for heavy air and 6½ inches (165 mm) for light air, which is three full turns difference on each adjuster. My crew can adjust them with ease by standing on the boom before the start.

Boom

It is essential that the boom you use is both light and stiff. The large thin-walled sections give the best results. Be sure to choose a boom that swivels on a round pin gooseneck and also has adjustable take-off points for both vang and mainsheet.

Try also to choose a triangular section with its apex uppermost so that when pushed out to the shroud the foot of the sail rests right up against it. This is very important for running downwind and essential if the class rules forbid shroud levers or shroud adjustment.

Rig controls

1   *Mast step.* This must be a perfect fit with the heel tenon or the mast will rotate, again spoiling spreader settings.

2   *Mast chocks.* Chocks in front of the mast at gate level restrict mast bend. Although restricting bend at deck level is not quite as effective as at spreader height, chocks are essential to any hog-stepped boat that is forbidden the use of either a 'strut' or 'lower shrouds' (e.g. the 470). Their primary function is to control bend low down in the spar, and they are particularly useful for fine control of the mast while on the race course. Adding chocks has the following effects:

- Decreases mast bend.
- Increases rig tension by making the mast straighter, thereby adding height to the rig

MAST CHOCKS AND STRUTS

**Too many chocks give too straight a mast (top left).
Too few chocks give too much bend (top right). Right:
on this boat mast chocks have been replaced by a
wire and ferrule arrangement, while (centre) a strut
controls mast bend low down, working against the
thrust from the boom.**

which, in turn, increases tension on the standing rigging.
- Reduces the rake of the mast.
- Reduces the load on the spreaders making them less effective which, in turn, lets the mast bend a little more higher up.

(Note that removing chocks has the opposite effect).

3   *Struts and lower shrouds.* The *strut* is a tube, usually built from aluminium or stainless steel, that attaches to the mast at gooseneck level and protrudes forward at an angle of 45 degrees to the spar, fastening onto a sliding car for adjustment on the foredeck.

Lower shrouds are stainless wires exiting from the mast at gooseneck level and attaching onto muscle boxes or purchases below the deck at the shroud base.

Both struts and 'lowers' control the mast in the same way as chocks but are much more effective in doing the job, as they are in a more advantageous position higher up the spar, working directly against the thrust from the boom.

4   *Spreaders.* As most people now know, increasing the length of the spreaders stiffens the mast sideways and angling them forward stiffens it fore and aft. It's important, however, that you also know the other effects available from your spreaders.

With your spreaders set (on a 470, Fireball or 505) with 3 inches (75 mm) of deflection sideways and 1 inch (25 mm) forward of the string line between hounds and deck, and with 350 lb (160 kg) of tension on the forestay, you will have 3 to 4 inches (75-100 mm) of pre-bend in the mast. If you then wanted to increase the bend you could do one or all of the following:

- Increase the tension.
- Angle the spreaders aft.
- Increase the spreader lengths.

(To decrease mast bend, reverse these adjustments).

By adding more and more tension you would keep on bending the spar until the spreader tips came into line with the string. After that your mast would carry on bending simply under compression without actually increasing rig tension. You would also begin to 'bend' your boat and so would increase its rocker (very slowly in most boats) and generally run the risk of breaking all your equipment.

It is, therefore, wise to decide on a sensible tension that will keep jib luff sag to a minimum and, while not forgetting the use of tension as a bending device, concentrate more on spreader deflections to achieve desired pre-bend and stiffness.

Once you have decided on the tension required

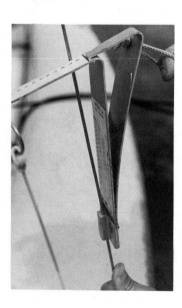

Far left: a tension meter is the best way of checking and reproducing rig tension. Near left: the shroud adjustment on this boat is quick and simple.

MAINSHEET OR VANG?

1 The mainsheet pulls downwards: increasing tension closes the leech and gives more power.

2 The vang pulls downwards *and* forwards; increasing tension gives a twisted leech and flattens the main low down — which is useful in strong winds.

— generally a minimum of 250 lb (115 kg) and a maximum of 400 lb (180 kg) — make sure that with full bend your spreaders are still extended at least 1½ inches (40 mm) outwards to keep side bend down to a minimum when out on the course.

If you have no idea of how much pre-bend you should start with, then ask your sailmaker how much luff curve he has put on the sail and begin with 25 per cent less. This is only a guide, but it will be a good starting point, and remember that it is in the lightest of winds that you need maximum bend.

5 *Rigging and spreader size.* Make sure your shrouds are at least 3 mm in diameter, as any less will stretch when loaded and your spreaders won't be as effective. The same goes for your spreaders: if they can bend, then change them for stiffer ones.

6 *Hounds position.* Unless your class of boat goes fast with a bendy top-mast, make sure your shrouds are located at the maximum height allowed by class rules. Your forestay or jib halyard sheave should then be positioned at exactly the same height or, if not, as close as rules permit. If

it is higher you will get reverse bend when loaded, and if it is below you will get pre-bend, especially high up in the spar. Your trapeze wires should be no further than 4 inches (100 mm) above the shrouds — any higher and your mast will start developing an S-bend sideways. The only advantage in moving them higher is to stiffen the top-mast sideways — this should not be necessary if the correct section is used.

7   *Boom thrust.* Sheeting the mainsail by the mainsheet pulls the boom downwards which, in turn, bends the mast. Using the vang to control the vertical height of the boom not only pulls the boom downwards but also pushes it forwards (due to the angle of the vang) directly into the mast at gooseneck level. Control of bend can, therefore, be regulated in two ways:

- The vang increases low-down bend.
- The mainsheet spreads bend more evenly.

Moving the mainsheet blocks forwards towards the mast again reduces low bend — moving them aft increases it.

Jib

If allowed by class rules, always use the same luff rod on all your jibs. Note that a rod is better than wire because it stretches less. You can then guarantee repeating rake and settings no matter which sail you use. Make sure the rod can slide up into the luff of the sail and be tied off easily at both ends. Tie the head first (the tack end is adjusted before the start). Arrange the lashing so that when maximum tension is applied down the luff the tack just touches the foredeck, reducing turbulence under the sail. This is called 'endplating'.

Hoist the sail and tension the rig, making sure the sail can turn or swivel around the wire once it has been tied off at both ends. Sheet the sail in hard and check that the foot also just touches the foredeck. Arrange the jib tracks or fairleads so that when in their midway position the jibsheet bisects the clew of the jib. Make sure they have enough travel so that the sail can be sheeted hard along the foot or the leech.

If the foot does not rest on the deck then check

The jib foot should lie along the foredeck; this reduces the turbulence under the sail.

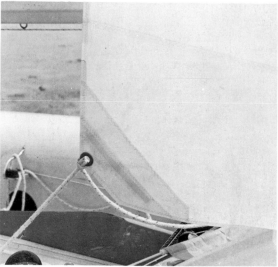

With the lead in its mid position the jibsheet bisects the clew.

Forward sheeting for medium winds.

Medium position for light winds.

Aft sheeting for strong winds.

ALTERING THE JIBSHEET LEAD

Above: position telltales on the jib at one-third, half and two-thirds luff length.

either the mast rake (more will bring the clew down) or the measurements your sailmaker has used; most class rules give only maximum luff and leech lengths, and it may be possible to lower the clew by reducing luff length.

The inboard/outboard position will vary from boat to boat, but generally you will need a wide sheeting angle for large overlapping genoas (e.g. Flying Dutchman) and a narrow angle for small overlaps (e.g. Soling and Fireball). Again, check the top guys' boats and start from there.

Position the telltales 6 inches (150 mm) back from the luff at one-third, half, and two-thirds luff length. Use green ones on starboard and red on port, with the red 1 inch (25 mm) above the green so that there is never any confusion. Choose wool or any material that is light and will not stick to the sail when wet (like spinnaker cloth).

Mainsail

Battens. As a rule long battens (relative to mainsail width) should be tapered and short battens untapered.

Using tapered battens where the batten length is almost half the sail width is fine, because their inboard ends should still be following the sail's camber. However, if the batten is shorter than this, its full length is needed to keep the exit of the sail straight.

The top batten should never be tapered, due to high compression as it butts up against the mast. Any taper here would cause too much camber just behind the mast. Choose a softer top batten for medium airs and a stiffer one for light and heavy airs.

Mainsail controls. Hoist the sail up the mast and make sure the headboard rests level with the black band when tension is applied down the luff. Put the boom on the gooseneck and pull the outhaul out to the black band. You can then position the tack of the sail by tying a string around the mast and through the cringle, adjusting it until you find the position it takes up best without forming creases.

The luff of the sail should now be just slack and the foot bar tight, with both bolt ropes running correctly into their respective tracks. You are now ready to go afloat and fine-tune on the water.

1

2

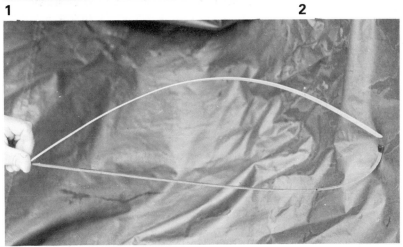

3

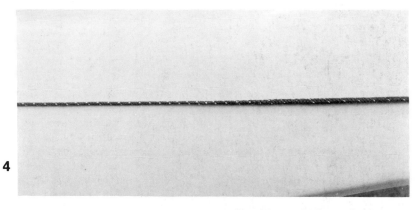

4

1 An alternative method of adjusting fore-and-aft
lead position.
2 The tack of the main is best held in place with rope.
Note the gooseneck in the correct position for the
black band.

3 Battens: untapered (top) for use in the top batten
pocket. Tapered (bottom) for use when the battens
are long compared with the width of the sail.
4 Tapered spinnaker sheet; the crew should never
have to handle the thin section.

3 Tuning on the water

BEATING IN MEDIUM WINDS

Choose a medium-air day to go out on your own to set your boat up. Set the fairleads in their middle position and pull in the jibsheet enough to make all three telltales lift at the same time. If the top one lifts before the bottom, then either move the car forward or sheet the sail harder. Moving the car forward makes the sail fuller and more powerful while sheeting harder does the reverse. The former would be good for rough water, the latter for smooth water. If the lowest telltale lifts first, then either move the car aft or sheet out.

When you have established a good position then mark your jibsheets so that you can repeat the settings from one tack to another.

Before setting your mainsail make sure that before applying any sheet tension your mast is just touching the chocks at deck level, and that there is enough wind for your crew either to hike flat out or, if in a trapeze boat, to be out on the wire.

Pull on enough cunningham so that the small creases behind the mast just disappear, and

enough outhaul so that a ridge of cloth begins to appear. Sheet the sail using the mainsheet and leave the vang slack. Pull enough tension on to make the telltale on the leech at the top batten just begin to 'break' or fall down. Sight up the sail and see if the mast is over-bending. If it is you will get big creases forming out of the luff from the half-height area, and you should move your spreaders far enough forward to make them just disappear. If there are no creases, move the spreaders aft until they appear, and then move them forward again until the creases just disappear.

Once your spreaders are in this position you are at a good starting point because you can then control bend more accurately via chocks or rig tension.

Developing more power

Sail the boat upwind and decide if you could handle more power from your sails. If you or your crew are not fully hiking or trapezing then you obviously can. Generally speaking the crew who are working the hardest to keep their boat upright are the fastest in medium airs as they are developing the most power from their sails. Power can be increased by:

- Bringing the traveller up to weather to get the boom closer to the centreline.
- Moving the jib cars forward and easing the sheet making the jib fuller.
- Adding chocks to make the mainsail deeper.
- Easing the cunningham.
- Easing the outhaul.

1 *Bringing the traveller up* will increase power, but be careful not to overdo it. It usually pays to flatten the base of the mainsail when the boom is on the centreline; this stops the leech pointing up to weather, causing drag. As the wind increases then pull the traveller up a little because the leech will be opening, and down when the wind drops

Marking your sheets is essential to enable you to repeat settings.

SETTING THE JIB
Check the jib slot and adjust the lead position and
sheet tension (see pages 22-3).

and the leech closes. Generally aim to keep the boom around 3 to 4 inches (75-100 mm) off the centreline, only letting it down more when you are overpowered in the gusts.

2   *Moving the jib cars forward* will result in a fuller sail with a tighter leech. The jibsheet must, therefore, be eased to keep the telltales flowing together. By adjusting both you will widen the slot between main and jib whilst creating a fuller shape. It will probably then pay to move the cars inboard to get back to the original slot width. Going to the extreme will result in too full a sail with too deep an entry and too round a back, the former stopping you pointing and the latter throwing air into the back of the mainsail choking the slot. Generally experiment until you have maximum power and good pointing ability.

3   *Adding chocks* makes the mainsail fuller, particularly in its lower half, and also by

straightening the mast makes the leech tighter. You will, therefore, get more power from the rig, but you will have to ease the mainsheet to keep the air flowing across the sail (keep the top telltale just flowing) and this in turn will stop you pointing quite as high as before. Putting in too many chocks will deepen the base of the sail excessively and backwinding will occur when the slot becomes choked. Again compromise until you feel you have plenty of power whilst still keeping good pointing ability.

4   *Easing the cunningham* right off will move the draft aft in the mainsail, which in turn will close the middle of the leech and give you more power. Reducing cunningham tension also straightens the top-mast which makes the sail fuller. Don't worry about the small creases appearing out of the luff; only pull on tension when you begin to be overpowered.

1

4

2

JIB CONTROL SETTINGS
When you have the jib set correctly, all the telltales should break together as you luff.
1 Lead too far forward.
2 Lead correct.
3 Lead too far aft.
4 Sheet too tight.
5 Sheet correct.
6 Sheet too loose.

3

5

6

5   *Easing the outhaul* dramatically increases camber in the lower half of the mainsail. Unfortunately the flow in the sail also moves back, and easing the outhaul too much will result in a closed lower leech and a choked slot. Therefore only use the outhaul as a fine power-on/off device, easing no more than 2 inches (50 mm) from bar tight; any more and the sail will stall, unless you let the traveller down sufficiently to keep the air flowing off the leech properly.

Feel on the helm

Weather helm is when the boat wants to point up into the wind. *Lee helm* is when the boat wants to point away from the wind. *Neutral helm* is when the boat wants to go in a straight line.

Firstly you must be sailing the boat level: that is, with the mast at right angles to the water when sighting from astern. You must also be correctly positioned in the boat to balance it fore and aft; i.e. close together, with the boat neither dragging its stern nor burying its bow.

Once you are happy that the boat is in fact level, then let go of the helm and see what happens. What you are looking for is a touch of weather helm. Both lee helm and neutral helm are disastrous. Lee helm forces you to push the tiller away, forming lift off the wrong side of the blade, and neutral helm means you gain no lift at all. Too much weather helm, however, makes your rudder work at too great an angle dragging sideways through the water creating excessive drag. The ways to alter 'helm feel' or balance are:

- Moving the heel of the mast.
- Raking the mast.
- Raking the centreboard.
- Moving the position of the centreboard.
- Raking the rudder.
- Altering the sails.

1   *Moving the heel of the mast* aft moves the whole mainsail aft, increasing weather helm in the same way as raking the mast. Your downwind performance should stay the same, and normally this would be the first step in altering the balance of the boat. The slot width fore and aft will increase, but only marginally.

2   *Raking the mast* aft moves the centre of effort of the rig back over the centre of the hull, thus pushing the stern to leeward and creating weather helm (see diagram below). This is fine, providing

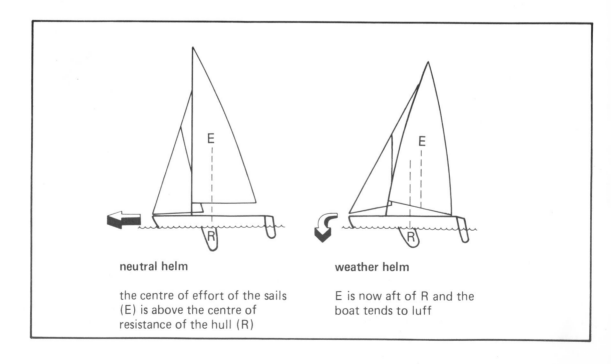

neutral helm

the centre of effort of the sails (E) is above the centre of resistance of the hull (R)

weather helm

E is now aft of R and the boat tends to luff

by doing so you don't lose out downwind. Also, as you rake the mast the distance between the mainsail and the jib becomes greater, creating a wider slot which would be good for heavy winds but not so desirable for light and medium airs.

3   *Raking the centreboard* forward or aft of vertical is really a tuning aid for use only in different wind strengths. You should therefore keep the leading edge of the foil either vertical or with 2 degrees of forward rake when beating in medium winds. You can then rake it aft in a breeze or further forward in light airs.

4   *Moving the position of the centreboard* in its case is a very effective way of altering balance. Providing you don't have a daggerboard, you should have at least 1 inch (25 mm) of tolerance allowable by class rules. Increase weather helm by simply moving the board's pivot bolt further forward.

5   *Raking the rudder* forward reduces helm, raking it aft increases helm. Again, start with the rudder vertical in medium winds so that you can introduce helm in light airs by raking aft and reduce helm in a breeze by raking forwards.

6   *Altering the sails:* a tight mainsail leech increases weather helm, as does a full main.

BEATING IN LIGHT WINDS

Once you are happy with your rig and the balance of the boat in medium airs, you can try to get some new settings for light and heavy breezes.

Make sure everything on your boat is calibrated: you are aiming to find and record fast settings for use in your first race or your two-boat tuning session. It is vital that you can change to new settings quickly, as the fastest boat on the course in 15 knots of wind will only remain in front if the crew adjusts the equipment when the wind changes to either 5 or 25 knots.

Having set up for just flat-out trapezing (fully powered-up conditions of, say, 6 to 15 knots), you must now learn how to change down a gear for 0 to 6 knots of wind. Firstly, you must understand what the rig should be doing. The air is very light in strength so it has little energy, and does not like sticking to or bending around large curves — your sails. If you make the sails too full they will simply stall, and you will either go slowly

Sight up the mast to check fore-and-aft bend, and that the mast is straight sideways (see page 26).

or you won't be able to point. The only way you can make full sails work in light airs is to keep them well eased with plenty of twist, i.e. jib sheeting cars right back and the boom well below the centreline. This, however, will not get you around the windward mark first in a championship race.

Assuming you are using one set of sails for all weathers you must, therefore, adapt them to suit the conditions:

- Pull the outhaul right out to the black band to flatten the base and the lower third of the sail.
- Remove all chocks from in front of the mast and angle your spreaders half an inch (12 mm) further aft than for your medium-air setting.

These adjustments alone will give you a much flatter sail which you will be able to sheet harder and closer than before, without closing the leech.

In these conditions you need to carry maximum mast bend and only begin to restrict it at gate level when your crew begins either to hike or trapeze. Until that point sheet harder and harder,

1　　　　　　　　**2**　　　　　　　　**3**

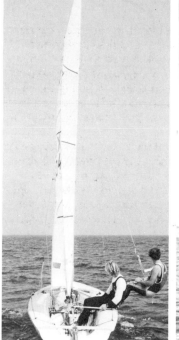

MAST BEND (above)

1 Too much bend (note the excessive creases); add more chocks.
2 Correct — chocks have been added until creasing is on the point of disappearing.
3 Too little bend; you will need to ease the mainsheet a long way to make the top telltale flow.

MAINSHEET (opposite)

1 Pull in the mainsheet until the top telltale is *just* flowing.
2 Too much mainsheet and the leech stalls (shown by the top telltale breaking).
3 Too little mainsheet and you lose power and pointing ability — although, confusingly, all the telltales flow.

OUTHAUL

The outhaul should be tight (far left), so the foot is well creased. If the outhaul is eased (near left), the flow over the lower leech breaks down (shown by the bottom telltale drooping). You then have to drop the traveller excessively to reattach the flow.

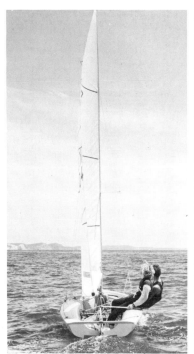 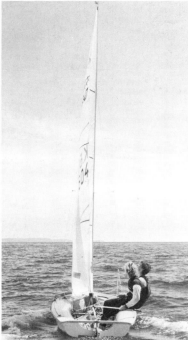 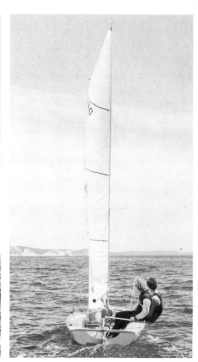

1 **2** **3**

keeping the top telltale just on the break. As soon as your crew gets on the trapeze you will again have to sheet harder and, at the same point, you will see creases forming out of the luff due to overbending of the spar. At this stage add a small chock (3/8 inch or 10 mm) to remove the creasing.

No cunningham needs to be used (this would pull the flow forward, which you don't want for light air), and leave the vang slack. Keep the boom close to the centreline and ease the sheet in and out in the puffs, leaving the traveller cleated.

The jib cars will have to be moved back. Sit down to leeward to study the flow over the jib. Arrange the sheeting so that the sail is as flat as possible with a small amount of twist. The telltales should still all be streaming together. A fairly wide slot is needed so as not to choke the weak airflow, so sheet tension can be relatively slack.

Ease the cunningham on the jib until you see small creases forming out of the luff. This will make the sail easier to 'read' and will enable the flow to move aft in the sail.

Once you are happy with the rig, sail the boat upright and let go of the tiller. In light breezes you should have more helm than in medium winds. Rake your centreboard to its maximum forward position — 10 degrees is plenty — and achieve more helm if needed by raking the rudder approximately 10 degrees aft. If you have a fixed rudder it would pay to get a special light-weather design.

Remember that all balance tuning relies on the skill of the crew in keeping the boat level. Any heel to leeward will confuse your objectives.

Finally, note that you should *not* slacken rig tension for light airs. Keep the same tension as for medium winds (the only changes are made in strong winds).

Through the gears

As the wind builds into flat-out trapezing conditions of 6 to 15 knots begin to adjust your settings to power up the rig. Firstly the mast bend will need to be reduced to prevent the mainsail from inverting (i.e. major creases forming from clew to mid-mast). Before altering the spreader settings, try adding a small ⅜ inch (10 mm) chock at deck level. This will immediately give you more power by creating a deeper mainsail with a tighter leech. As the boat is not yet overpowered you are still looking for height (pointing ability) rather than speed. Therefore, keep the mainsheet cleated and play the traveller in the gusts so that leech tension is maintained.

The jib tracks will have to be moved forward to increase the jib's depth, and ease the sheet out to keep all three telltales breaking together. If you can still handle more power, then ease the outhaul 1 inch (25 mm) being careful to avoid 'hooking' the leech and stalling the lower third of the sail.

Pull on a little jib cunningham to stop the flow moving too far aft and closing the leech. Leave the mainsail's cunningham slack until you become overpowered.

BEATING IN HEAVY WINDS

As the wind picks up to 15 knots and over, you will have to start releasing power from the rig.

1   *Rake.* Due to increased sheet and vang tension the mainsail will now be flatter with more twist. It will also be eased further out from the centreline, and consequently weather helm will be reduced. You can now afford to rake the mast further aft to compensate for the movement in the rig's 'balance'. More rake in the stronger airs is beneficial because it increases the gap between the leech of the jib and the luff of the mainsail, creating a wider slot for the increased wind speed to pass through. Rake also lowers the clews on both sails which reduces their height above deck, resulting in a reduction of heeling force. Therefore increase the aft rake of the mast by 4 inches (100 mm) measuring from the top of the spar to the lower edge of the transom.

2   *Spreaders.* Because the mast has been raked aft, the position of the spreaders in relation to the shrouds will also have moved back, which bends the mast more. You must, therefore, move them forward to keep pre-bend in the spar constant. However, as you are now using more vang tension, your mast will be bending more and you will have to move the spreaders further forward still to prevent the sail from inverting. My 470 and 505

spreaders are angled 1 inch (25 mm) further forward for heavy airs.

3   *Chocks.* Again, as rake is increased, the distance between the mast and the chocks becomes greater, so you must add more chocks to keep the pre-bend the same. As the wind builds stronger, however, it may pay you to remove a small chock — say ¼ inch (6 mm). This will let the mast bend low down, which will in turn flatten the lower half of the sail and open up the slot.

4   *Rig tension.* If your boat is strong enough, and capable of taking more rig tension, increase the load on the forestay by 15 per cent. This will keep jib luff sag constant, which is a must, as any sag in the luff will create a fuller entry and a tighter leech — the opposite of your requirements in strong winds.

Remember also that any increase in mast bend results in a decrease in rig tension as the hounds become lower. A decrease in mast bend has the opposite effect,

5   *Cunningham.* Gradually apply more cunningham as the breeze increases. The amount of load that you can put on the luff will depend largely on the type of bolt rope used by the sailmaker in manufacture. The stretchier the rope is, the more control you will have over the sail.

Increasing the cunningham tension will 'pull' the camber in the sail forward, which in turn makes the leech of the sail flatter enabling the air to flow off the rig more easily. On a spar that is already bent, added cunningham will also increase mast bend, particularly at the tip. This is also helpful in flattening the head of the sail and further reducing power.

Pull on the jib cunningham until a ridge of cloth just appears behind the luff wire. This again will keep the flow well forward and, more importantly, will keep the leech of the sail open in its head for the wind to escape from.

6   *Fairleads.* Move the fairleads forward until the top telltale is breaking on the weather side before the middle one, and the middle one before the lower one. You can then sheet the sail a little harder along the foot, which will flatten its base without closing the leech near the head. The sail should be twisted well off and the sheet eased in the gusts to increase the slot width and prevent the mainsail from backwinding.

TRAVELLER
Near right: begin with the boom 2 inches (50 mm) below the centreline (the traveller will need to be to weather to achieve this). In stronger winds (far right) ease the traveller down; but in medium winds a low traveller reduces power and pointing ability.

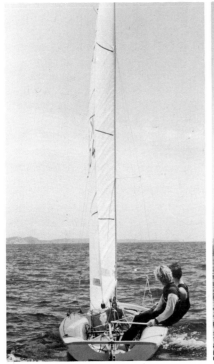

CUNNINGHAM
Far left: begin with the cunningham off. Only pull it on when you begin to be overpowered. If you do this too soon (near left) the flow moves too far forward and the head of the sail opens too early.

7 *Centreboard.* Rake the centreboard aft between 10 degrees and 15 degrees depending on wind strength. This will reduce the board's total surface area and also reduce weather helm, so that when a gust hits the boat will drive forward rather than turn into the wind.

8 *Rudder.* Rake the rudder forward by 5 degrees. This will reduce the 'weight' in the helm making steering easier, particularly through heavy seas.

9 *Mainsheet, traveller and vang.* Transfer from using the mainsheet to control the twist of the sail, to the vang. Set the traveller in its central position and play the mainsheet in the gusts.

Using vang tension will increase bend low down in the spar which will flatten the sail and open the slot. Mainsail leech tension will be reduced as the mast bends more and the sail becomes flatter.

Control the lateral position of the boom using the mainsheet and use the vang to control power, easing it to make the sail fuller in the lulls and tightening it for the gusts. If the wind drops so light that your crew is beginning to bend his

FULLY TUNED SAILS

When fully tuned for medium winds the sails should look like the ones shown in the two photographs at left.

In light airs they should look like the sails shown in the bottom row, opposite page; while in strong winds they should look like the ones shown below.

Altering the jib cunningham. More tension is used as the wind increases, to keep the flow forward and open the head of the sail.

knees, then do not hesitate to release the cunningham, and transfer back to mainsheet tension immediately.

10   *Outhaul.* This should be pulled all the way out to the black band to flatten the base of the sail.

REACHING WITHOUT A SPINNAKER

To achieve good speed on a reach in medium winds you must make the sails fuller than for upwind work.

Ease the cunningham off completely and release the outhaul until you see vertical creases forming out of the bottom of the sail.

Ease the vang until the top telltale is just flowing. The more vang tension you use, the flatter and tighter-leeched the sail will become. A tight leech is good for reaching as it generates maximum power by preventing the air from escaping out of the sail too soon. However, to achieve a tight leech you require plenty of vang tension which will bend the mast and flatten the sail just when you need maximum fullness. You must, therefore, hold the spar as straight as possible because any bend will result in a loss of speed.

Rake. If you have adjustable shrouds, then ease both off and pull on the jib halyard until the mast

is upright. Leaving the chocks in their upwind position will result in the mast bend inverting at deck level, giving you a stiffer spar and a more powerful mainsail.

Without shroud adjustment you cannot rake the mast forward. Instead, ease the rig tension via the jib halyard. This will reduce any pre-bend in the mast and, again, give you a fuller mainsail. Be careful not to ease the jib halyard so far that the rig becomes slack as this will add 'aft rake' which is slow on the reach.

Centreboard. Lift the centreboard gradually, stopping as you feel the boat begin to slip sideways. Keep as much area of the board in the case as possible to reduce its surface area, which will increase speed providing that the boat is going straight and not slipping sideways.

Balance. In some classes, weather helm or lee helm can be experienced on a reach. If you are trimming your sail correctly and are getting lee helm, then use more centreboard; use less if you are getting weather helm. The alternative is to heel the boat to windward when you have weather helm and to leeward with lee helm.

Fairleads. As the jib is eased out for the reach, the head of the sail twists open and the sail must be oversheeted in the base to keep the top working. Therefore move the fairleads forward to keep all three telltales breaking together. If you have the facility to move the fairleads outboard then do so to increase the width of the slot. This will enable the mainsail to be let out further before the jib backwinds it.

If you have an adjustable cunningham then ease it off until horizontal creases appear out of the luff. Doing this will close the head and give the sail more fullness, working in much the same way as the boom outhaul does with the main.

Light wind adjustments

Basic settings for light-air reaching are the same as for medium winds. If the wind drops very light, put more bend into the mast and keep the vang slack so that the air can flow across the sail and escape from the leech without stalling.

Get your crew to hold the clew of the jib up to keep the leech open, and out to keep it clear of the mainsail.

Raise the centreboard until you have just

enough 'bite' to stop you slipping away sideways, and rake the rudder blade aft by 10 degrees so that you can turn the boat faster at low speed. Both helm and crew should move their weight forward to lift the aft sections of the hull clear of the water to reduce drag. If the sails are not filling properly, heel the boat over to leeward to make them set through their own weight.

Heavy wind adjustments

When the wind increases to the point where you are overpowered, i.e. helm and crew are hiked or trapezing flat out and still having to ease sheets, then begin to flatten the sails off.

Pull the outhaul out to the black band and return the rake and tension to their upwind settings. Ease the vang off until you can hold the boat level and, when a gust hits, ease the jib before the mainsheet. Put enough centreboard down to keep the boat tracking in a straight line and, if you are still overpowered, pull both cunninghams back on to open leeches still further in the heads of both sails.

To de-power further, move the jib fairleads further aft to 'dump' the top of the sail and lift the centreboard so that instead of heeling the boat slips sideways in the gusts.

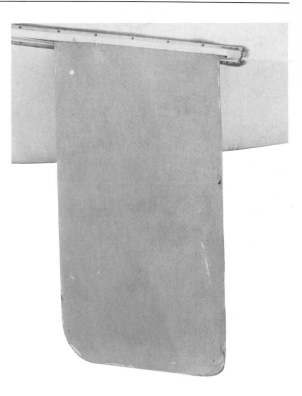

When beating, start with the leading edge of the centreboard raked forward 2 degrees. Rake the board aft (as shown above) as the wind increases. On a reach or run keep the maximum amount of board in the case.

RUNNING DOWNWIND WITHOUT A SPINNAKER

In medium airs the wind should be strong enough to promote marginal planing and your best course will be dead downwind to the mark. With the wind directly behind you the sails must be set to present the greatest projected area available.

Outhaul. Pull this out almost all the way to the black band, avoiding creating a crease above the boom. This will give you maximum foot length and increase sail area.

Rake. If you have shroud adjusters, let the windward one off until the mast is vertical in the boat. This again will increase area by adding height to the rig. Let the leeward shroud off enough to allow the boom to square off at right angles to the centreline of the boat. Doing this will effectively increase boom length and projected area.

Cunningham. Ease both jib and mainsail cunninghams right off.

Vang. Play the vang in the gusts and lulls, keeping the last 12 inches (0.3 metre) of the top batten parallel with the boom. Easing the vang off too much will result in a loss of power as the wind flows out of the head too easily. Too much vang will do the opposite by stalling the upper half of the sail.

Centreboard. Raise the centreboard until the boat becomes unstable (rocking from side to side). Try to steer the boat with heel so that minimum rudder movement need be used. Heeling the boat to leeward will make the boat luff; heeling to windward will make the boat bear away.

Never raise the board all the way into the case: less water will enter when the board is between the slot tapes.

1

2

3

Jib. Goosewing the jib using the longest pole allowed by class rules. If there is no limit, then aim for the foot of the sail to be taut and at right angles to the centreline of the boat. Arrange the pole's fixing on the mast so that the clew cannot 'sky' in the gusts. If it does a loss of power will occur when the wind spills out of the head of the sail. Again, clew height can be determined by keeping all three telltales breaking together.

Light wind adjustments

Set the boat up in the same way as for medium winds, again concentrating on minimum centreboard and minimum rudder movement. Ease the vang off so that you have more twist in the sail head to keep the weak air flowing across and out of the upper leech. If the wind drops lighter you will have to head up to a broad reach and adjust settings as for light-air reaching.

Heavy wind adjustments

As the breeze picks up to continuous planing conditions, keep the boat headed dead downwind and increase vang tension to maintain correct leech twist (top batten lined up with the boom). If the vang is too slack the top of the sail will twist away to leeward and the boat will become unstable, with the risk of a capsize. You will also need more centreboard to increase stability.

In extreme conditions it is worth while tying a knot in the mainsheet to prevent the boom from touching the shroud. This will reduce the chance of either breaking the mast or the boom, as when the boom hits the shroud it acts as a lever (with the shroud as fulcrum) forcing the mast aft.

Spars that break at gooseneck level and vang take-off positions are generally the result of neglecting to tie such a knot, or are caused during a capsize when the boom hits the water and forces the mast out of column.

RAKING THE RUDDER
1 In light winds angle the rudder blade aft to increase feel.
2 In medium winds adjust rake so the helm is light when the boat is upright.
3 In strong winds rake the blade forward to make the boat easier to steer.

4 The spinnaker

Your choice of spinnaker depends on several factors:

- The type of boat you sail.
- The course you are racing on.
- The venue of the race.
- Whether you use a spinnaker chute or bags.

1 *Type of boat.* In the past, almost all classes of boat used maximum or near-maximum width spinnakers. The classic example is the 12-metre: in 1958 'Sceptre' had a kite 90 feet (27 metres) wide, whereas the current popular width is 44 feet (13 metres).

In almost all performance dinghies the trend has been the same, with luff and foot dimensions remaining maximum and a reduction in the half-height measurement. The reason for this development is largely due to the introduction of the Olympic course, with two reaching legs and only one run. The full-size running spinnaker nearly always loses out to the smaller reaching job around the full course.

It is on the reaches that the smaller kite comes into its own. As it is narrower, the overlap between spinnaker and mainsail is reduced, creating a wider, more efficient slot; this enables the mainsail to be eased out further before backwinding occurs. On the run the smaller kite seldom loses out: it is more stable and easier to set, with the advantage in light airs of weighing less and needing less wind to fill it.

Unless your class of boat has a very small spinnaker it generally makes sense to go for the better reaching kite, particularly if you are down on crew weight.

Spinnaker pole length is also a factor. In the 505, for example, which has an extremely long pole, you tend to have lee helm on the reach. A small spinnaker makes this worse. The solution is to have a reasonably wide kite (and to sail the boat heeled to leeward, with the centreboard raised further than usual).

2   *The course.* Olympic classes go through an angle of 90 degrees on their gybe mark, whereas Fireball championship courses are usually set with 60 degree wing marks. So on the 60 degree course use a smaller, flatter spinnaker.

3   *The venue.* The venue of the major championships you are aiming for will affect your choice. You should definitely go for a smaller kite at a heavy-air venue, and you might consider ordering a large spinnaker for a light-air series.

4   *Chute or bags.* Most proven fast dinghy spinnakers are now made using a cross-cut panel layout. Although vertical head, triradial and star-cut designs are all essential in the production of big-boat sails, these designs are not needed for smaller spinnakers. This is basically because dinghies use the same cloth weights as the 12-metres and maxis — there just isn't a lighter cloth available that will not rip under the conditions experienced around a dinghy course. So special

panel configurations to reduce stretch are not, therefore, required for small spinnakers, even when using 1/2-oz cloths.

The total weight of the sail is also a consideration, and the extra seams in a multi-panel design increase the spinnaker's weight.

I would personally always go for the conventional cross-cut 1/2-oz design, made from Dynac or other low-stretch material, in a boat without a spinnaker chute. For a boat with a chute, the best choice would be a 3/4-oz cross-cut made from a silicon-finished cloth, more for its slippery surface and water-shedding properties than for its pure cloth performance. It is essential when using a chute to be able to hoist and lower the sail quickly, and also for the spinnaker to shed water when hoisted (water constantly pours onto the sail when it is in the chute).

Setting the spinnaker

1   Your spinnaker halyard sheave should be as high as the class rules permit.
2   Arrange the halyard so the head flies 4 to 6 inches (100-150 mm) away from the mast. This will prevent the upper half of the mainsail being closed by the spinnaker.
3   The spinnaker pole should be to maximum length. Make sure the end fits tightly to the eye on the mast; any slop here will result in a reduction of length. If the class rules allow, position the eye on the mast so the pole is horizontal in its average position, giving maximum length.
4   The fairleads should be as far outboard as possible. As a rule the fairleads should be positioned as far aft as practicable, so that when sheeted for close reaching the distance between the clew and fairlead is maximised, allowing the sail to set further away from the rig. With the

Below: the spinnaker lead should be as far outboard as possible and as far aft as is practicable. Note that because the 470 boom is short, the leads shown here have to be forward of the transom to prevent the sheet riding over the boom.

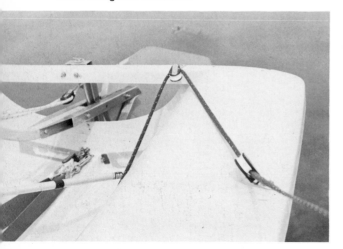

POLE HEIGHT ON A REACH
Opposite page — inset top and centre: with the pole too high the clew is too low and the leech closes. Inset, bottom: if the pole is set too low the luff becomes too rounded. Once the spinnaker is no longer symmetrical, speed drops. Main picture: this spinnaker is flying perfectly with the clews level.

REACHING IN STRONG WINDS
Above, top: when overpowered on a
spinnaker reach, aim to lose drive
from the main by easing the vang and
tensioning the cunningham. This has
been done in the bottom photo.

REACHING IN LIGHT WINDS
As the wind drops you will find the
pole is too high (above, top). Lower it
until the clews are level (bottom). The
same technique can be used if you
need to pinch up to the mark.

fairlead well aft the leech will never be put under excessive load and will not be closed by leech tension.

If you have an extremely wide boat, however, it can pay to bring the fairleads forward to the position of maximum beam to increase the width of the slot.

Reaching in medium winds

Pole height. In these conditions you require full power from all three sails to generate sufficient speed. The pole's height is determined by the vertical profile designed into the spinnaker. Try watching your own boat from a tender to study the effects of various pole heights.

The luff of the sail should be breaking just above mid-height when the lower half of the sail is vertical to the water surface.

If your fairlead, pole height and spinnaker

POLE ANGLE ON THE RUN
1 Pole too far aft (the jib interferes with air flow out of the base of the spinnaker).
2 Pole correct.
3 Pole too far forward (drive is lost).

design are correct, both clews should also be flying level with each other.

As the reach becomes closer you will obviously have to sheet harder, resulting in the clew becoming lower than the tack. Unless you can move the fairlead aft, you will have to lower the pole to keep tack and clew level and the spinnaker symmetrical. Doing this will prevent the leech from closing and backwinding the mainsail.

As the reach becomes broader your sheet must be eased and the clew will rise. You must now raise the pole to keep tack and clew level. If the clew is higher than the tack a reduction in power will occur, working in the same way as moving the jib fairleads aft.

Pole angle. Clew height can also be controlled by pole angle. That is, as the tack is swung forward, the sheet can be eased, which in turn opens the leech, creating a wider slot. Swinging the pole aft has the reverse effect. It is, therefore, essential to adjust both height and angle constantly as the wind direction varies down your straight-line course to the mark. Play the sheet in and out all the time, keeping the luff on the verge of collapsing. If the wind goes forward, drop the pole down and forward — and vice versa, if the wind goes aft.

1   2   3

1

2

1

2

3

3

POLE HEIGHT ON THE RUN (above)
1 Pole too high (clews not level).
2 Correct — note the base of the spinnaker is vertical and the clews level.
3 Pole too low — the spinnaker is unsymmetrical and the base has drooped.

MAINSAIL TRIM ON THE RUN (left)
1 The vang is tensioned correctly — the top batten is parallel to the boom.
2 The vang is too loose; in light winds you will notice a loss in power, while in strong winds the boat will roll.
3 Here the vang is too tight, preventing air from flowing over the top of the sail.

Reaching in heavy winds

Until you are overpowered, set the spinnaker in the same way as for medium winds. As the breeze freshens, swing the pole forward onto the forestay and ease the sheet so that the luff is curling all the time. As the breeze increases, gradually drop the pole which, in turn, will open up the leech as the clew becomes higher relative to the tack. Ease the vang right off. This 'dumps' air out of the mainsail and also lets the spinnaker sheet rise higher (in most boats the boom is so low that the sheet is held down under it).

Reaching in light winds

Again, keep both tack and clew level. As the wind goes lighter the clew will drop due to insufficient force available to lift the weight of the sail. You must then lower the pole, which will straighten the luff leaving less unsupported cloth for the air to fill and support. Use the lightest of sheets because their weight alone will prevent the sail from lifting.

Running in medium winds

On the run, aim to present as much spinnaker area to the wind as possible without stalling the sail.

Pole height.
- Set the pole to keep the clews level.
- Also set the pole so the centre seam of the spinnaker, from half-height downwards, is vertical.

Pole angle.
- Swinging the pole too far aft will bring the kite too close to the jib, preventing air flowing out of its base.
- Swinging the pole too far forward will result in a loss of projected area because the clews come closer togther.

Sometimes the centre seam of the spinnaker is correct and the luff breaks nicely just above mid-height *but* the clew persists in flying higher than the tack. Rather than lift the pole, pull down on the leeward twinning line to keep the clew down (the twinning line is now acting like a barber-hauler).

Running in light winds

As the wind fades the spinnaker will begin to collapse. Lower the pole to reduce the amount of unsupported cloth and get your crew down to leeward to hold the clew up, preventing its own weight and that of the sheet from working against the wind's weak force.

Another good trick is to have an open block fastened under the boom, just forward of the mainsheet blocks, for the sheet to pass over in light conditions. This reduces the weight on the clew and allows your crew to stay up to weather, taking the sheet directly from the boom.

Running in heavy winds

Set the sail as in medium winds until conditions become severe. In the strongest of breezes beware of setting the sail either to leeward or windward of the boat's centreline. With the pole too far aft a capsize to windward is on the cards; with it too far forward a broach followed by a capsize is likely.

Set the pole higher than before to let air escape out of the upper leeches and the base. Again use the leeward twinning line to prevent the clew from riding too high.

5   Two-boat tuning

Be sure before choosing your 'sparring partner' that he or she is reliable and is not going to fool around playing games. Ideally, choose a good friend who is of the same standard as yourself. It is important that you respect the other's sailing ability but, at the same time, feel that you can outsail them come the event you are both striving for. If there is no one of your own standard then always pick someone who is better. In that way you can always learn something. Agree between yourselves that so many days or weeks before the championships all cooperation will cease, but until that day you will both help each other as much as possible. The whole purpose of two-boat tuning is to raise the performance of both boats to

a stage where you do not mind which of the two you sail. It is only when you have this arrangement that complete trust can be evolved between yourself and your opponent.

If you happen to have two boats of your own, it is unlikely that you will find a sailor from another class who is sufficiently in touch with your type of boat to be of use. He will neither have the skill, the practice nor the desire to be fully competitive in a tune-up session.

Be sure to pick someone of your standard with a boat as competitive as your own. Before you embark on your first session, agree that your objectives are to evaluate speed and not individual skills. There is no point, for instance, in the

leeward boat sailing higher and slower than he normally would just to prove that he can 'squeeze' the weather boat out — unless that is your test.

Set the boats up in the dinghy park as you would normally for a race. Go out and be sure that the wind and tide are constant across your tune-up area. It is pointless tuning in a shifty wind or in tidal waters.

Upwind

Give yourself a minimum distance of three miles (5 km) to conduct a worthwhile test. Position the boats three to four lengths apart, with their bows level when head to wind. Set out with the weather boat calling the 'off', and sail on one tack as if you were going up the beat in a race. Don't take any notice of the other boat or this will spoil the test, e.g. if you are to weather and the leeward boat is pointing higher, you might be tempted to steer the same course; resist this, and sail your normal course.

Sail the boats until either one gives the other bad air or until the boats get too far apart. When separated the leeward boat should tack to clarify the gain or loss. Repeat the exercise to be certain of the conclusion and then swap positions, with the leeward boat now to windward. If the result is still the same you have a worthwhile conclusion, as there is obviously no tide or wind difference.

Raising the slower boat's performance

The faster boat's settings must now remain the same, and all effort is concentrated on getting the slower boat up to speed. This can be a frustrating exercise if your boat is the faster, but equalising performance is essential for the long-term programme because you cannot improve your own speed until this is achieved.

Initially check on the position of all controls — vang, traveller, chocks, spreaders, etc. If you still cannot achieve equal speed, swap jibs, then mainsails. Keep on switching equipment until you find the faster piece of gear. In the unlikely event of the same boat still being faster, your only option will be to buy a new hull or constantly allow for this speed difference.

As soon as you have raised the slower boat's performance you can begin to develop some speed gains. Line the boats up again with one boat staying constant while the other adjusts a setting. Be sure to alter only one setting at a time so as not to confuse the reason for a change in speed. Once a gain has been established, repeat it on the other boat so that the two work up in speed together.

Gradually go through all your settings until you have tested every permutation. You can then begin trying new sails and spars to look for even more speed.

Reaching

The process can now be repeated on the reach. Position one of the boats two lengths behind and one length to windward of the other. Make sure the boat behind is out of the leader's wash and not on her wind. The leading boat determines the direction by cleating the spinnaker and steering the boat to its luff. The boat behind should keep a constant distance to windward. Both boats should keep rudder movement to a minimum, only adjusting to stay on course. Crews should move just enough to keep heel constant, and techniques to promote surfing should be avoided.

Running

Again the tuning process is similar. Position one boat one length behind and three lengths to leeward of the other. The leading boat should steer a very accurate compass course while the boat behind keeps a constant distance to leeward. When there is a change in wind direction do not update the compass course until you have informed the other boat and taken results of gains or losses to date.

6   The race

Pre-start

Try to arrange with your tune-up partner (or another boat of similar speed) to do some quick straight-line tuning before the start of the race. This will enable you to set your boat up for the conditions of the day. Simply feeling the strength of wind on your face and looking at the water will not give you an accurate enough gauge of the conditions.

Arrive in the starting area at least 45 minutes before the ten-minute gun. Set off on your own to decide if there is any wind sheer, current or wave pattern that will force you to have different settings on starboard than on port tack. In big boats with tall masts the wind is stronger and usually more veered at the top, forcing you to sail with more

twist in the sails on starboard than on port*. A dinghy mast is nowhere near as tall, but the same effect can sometimes apply.

If the tide is on your lee bow on starboard and your weather bow on port you will have less power on port tack, and your settings will have to be adjusted to compensate. The wave pattern may also be strange, giving you smoother water on one tack than on the other. Line up against your tune-up boat and sail a ten to fifteen-minute

---

* This effect is reversed in the southern hemisphere.

beat to get a feel for the conditions. Take note of the marks on both mainsail and jib sheets to give you the correct sheet tension the moment you hit the start line. Often at the start you are too busy steering and watching other boats to have time to look up at the sails, and it pays to be able to go to the correct sheet tensions immediately.

Run back down to the starting area and check that your spinnaker is packed properly and is dry.

The start

If possible, decide before the gun on the type of start you are going to make. If, for instance, you think it will pay to hold on to a long starboard tack off the line, then set up the boat for pointing. Once you have clear air you can readjust for pure speed. If, though, you want to get inshore or to one side of the course quickly, it will pay you to set up for fast straight-line speed, sacrificing a little pointing ability.

The beat

Once you are settled down and sailing in clear air, decide what your options are relative to the rest of the fleet and adjust settings accordingly. You might, for instance, be to leeward of the majority of the boats and would want to sail higher so as to stay in touch with the fleet. Or you might be to windward of the fleet, sailing on a lift; if so it would pay to capitalise on the shift and go for more speed to get over the majority of boats and into the next shift sooner. Either way you must be able to change gears quickly, without hesitation, and it is here that exact calibration and knowledge of your boat pays dividends.

If you are sailing towards a windward shore, anticipate the flat water ahead and prepare to flatten off your sails. If you see a patch of lighter wind ahead, anticipate the lull and ease sheets, vang, etc. to make full use of the change. It is in these situations that boat speed can give you a real advantage over your opponents.

The reach

Have your spinnaker sheets, vang controls, and mainsail and jib sheets marked for their approximate reaching positions. You can then round the top mark and set the spinnaker, knowing

**Know the wind angle at which your spinnaker
performs best. If it is designed for close reaching,
attack; if not, defend.**

that all three sails will be pulling immediately. Know the wind angle at which your spinnaker performs best. If the sail is designed for close reaching then attack; if not, defend. Attack boats by passing them to weather; defend by steering a straight course, ignoring faster boats that will pass you anyway, and keeping your own distance sailed to a minimum.

Second reach   It is seldom that both reaches are exactly the same. It is essential that you are familiar with how your spinnaker sets on a true 135 degree wind angle, so that you can tell if the wind has shifted. If it has swung just 5 degrees then it will make a difference of 10 degrees to your sail settings on the new gybe; knowing this, you can approach the gybe mark ready with the exact pole height and angle, centreboard and vang positions for the next reach.

Decide on your tactics for the second beat before you reach the gybe mark. If you wish to carry on on port tack you have three options:

- Go high and stay clear of the boat ahead's lee-bow effect.
- Reach off to clear your air to leeward.
- Put in a short 'hitch' to clear your wind.

Your tactic here will depend on the boat ahead and how she sails. If you know the skipper is a

'stuffer' you can then adjust settings immediately either to reach off and break through to leeward, or to tack. Either way, decide before the mark and set up your boat accordingly.

The run

Before rounding the weather mark decide on the course you are going to take down the run. Ease the vang, cunningham and outhaul before the rounding and have your spinnaker sheets on their marked positions to make for a faster hoist. If you find boats are gaining by running squarer then check your board to see if you can raise it more. Keep the boom pushed hard out against the shroud and if you wish to sail still lower then ease the leeward shroud off more to keep the boom at right angles to the wind direction.

The finish

As soon as you cross the finish line, stop and write down all your settings and the changes you have made during the race. Once ashore you can copy these numbers into your log book for future use.

Troubleshooting

Your boat does not point...

CHECK:

Leech tension & twist

As a rule an open leech will produce good speed, and a closed or tight leech good height. A combination of the two is what you are after, but a lack of pointing ability often means that the mainsail leech is too open.

Mainsail leech. Try getting off your boat and into a tender to study your sail and compare it with faster boats. If it is twisting more and the design of the sail is the same as the opposition, then your problem lies in the way you are controlling the mast. Check that fore-and-aft bend is not excessive. A sure sign will be creases forming between the clew and the middle of the mast. If this is happening, more mainsheet or vang tension will only increase bend, flatten the sail and open the leech even more.

To cure the bend try adding an extra chock. If this does not work then angle the spreaders farther forward. Keep the top telltale on the break, and if you still get creases forming out of the luff before the top telltale 'breaks', your mast is still over-bending. Continue to angle the spreaders forward, adding chocks at the same time to keep the bend even until you have the top telltale working with the mast. Make sure that your boom is no more than 3 to 4 inches (75-100 mm) below the centreline.

Jib leech. Check that your jib leech is not too open by studying the telltales. Pointing will suffer if the top weather telltale is breaking before the lower ones. To cure the problem, sheet harder in smooth water and move the cars forward in waves.

Rig tension

Your jib will be cut for a given amount of forestay sag. If the rig is too slack the luff will sag more than it is designed to do, resulting in too full an entry in the sail. If this happens pointing will be poor, unless you sail with the front of the jib aback.

You can get an idea of how round the entry should be by feeling the boat's 'power response'. If you find the jib is constantly lifting when you point at the same angle as the rest of the fleet, then it is certainly too full. If, however, you find a big reduction in power when you point high enough to make the luff 'break' you have too fine an entry. Increase rig tension to cure the former, reduce it to cure the latter. You may, however, be happy with the rig tension as regards mast stiffness and pre-bend. If so, it is quite simple for your sailmaker to re-cut the jib. When you are satisfied with the modification a new sail can be ordered.

Outhaul	Try easing the outhaul to bring a little more fullness into the bottom of the sail, which will in turn tighten the leech. You should notice an immediate increase or decrease in speed.
Mast side bend	Check that all fittings dealt with earlier are secure — spreaders not moving, heel tenon tight, mast tight in partners, etc. Give the helm to your crew and sight up the mast when sailing to windward. Any side bend between the deck and the hounds will affect speed. Pointing will be poor if the middle of the spar is bending up to weather. This will happen when the spreaders are too long, or when they are too short combined with incorrect shroud tension. Firstly check the tension of both shrouds. With your crew on the trapeze it is possible for the leeward shroud to be tighter than the weather one. If this is the case the leeward spreader will take over and push the mast to windward, opening the slot and reducing power. The mainsail will also become flatter with the leech opening sooner, and pointing will suffer. To cure the problem either shorten the spreaders or increase rig tension until the weather shroud is as tight as the leeward one. If the mast is bending to weather *without* your crew on the trapeze, the problem will lie in the spreaders being too short or the rig tension too slack. If the spreaders are too short the tension in the shrouds will not be sufficient to hold the mast in column as the weather spreader tries to force the weather shroud out of line. If rig tension is too loose the same will happen, even with correct spreader length. Try to solve the problem by firstly increasing tension and, if that doesn't work, increase the spreader lengths leaving the fore-and-aft angle the same.
Centreboard	*Stiffness.* Try and find out how the leaders in your class are constructing their centreboards. It is likely that they are using stiffer boards than yours. Any flexibility in the foil is fine in a breeze but will be disastrous in medium airs when you are searching for power to help you point (the centreboard works in much the same way as the mast: as it bends it reduces power). Test the board's stiffness by turning the boat on its side and pushing the board around to judge its flexibility. If you feel you could do better, go away and acquire a stiffer type. *The section.* This book was not written to discuss ultimate foil sections. However, the fundamental rule is — if in doubt make the leading edge rounder. A sharp leading edge, if working correctly, will be faster than a round edge. High-speed sailing craft such as catamarans have sharper foils than slower boats, simply because they go faster and make less leeway. If, however, your board is too sharp it will stall in much the same way that

continued

Centreboard
continued

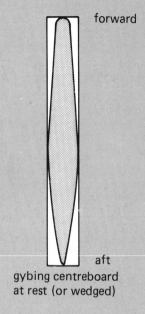

forward

aft

gybing centreboard
at rest (or wedged)

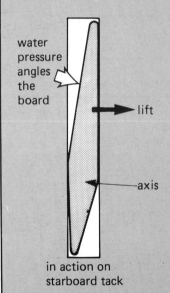

water
pressure
angles
the
board

lift

axis

in action on
starboard tack

the sails do, and if you are having problems pointing the first underwater area to attack is the leading edge.

You can experiment with your current section by making the entry rounder. If this doesn't work, gradually make it sharper until you find the best compromise. Plastic padding or other soft fillers are perfect for quick adjustments when the boat is on its side.

Gybing centreboards. Several classes have no restriction on the thickness and section of the centreboard. Shaping the head of the board into a diamond section will make the board pivot about its thickest point (see diagram). Maximum width must be at least 60 per cent aft to make sure that the leading edge of the board angles to windward under the water's pressure. The effect of a gybing board can be dramatic and, if it works correctly, the board will help the boat point higher. If, however, the board is gybing too far or pivoting on an axis that is too far forward, the section will stall and an increase in drag will occur.

To be safe, the first gybing board you try should have its axis (i.e. its maximum thickness) well aft, with its gybing angle no more than 2 degrees (4 degrees in total). If you can make this work it will be simple to experiment with greater angles and different axis positions on your existing board. As it seldom pays to 'gybe' the board in strong winds, it is essential to build a chock on the aft edge of the section just above the waterline, so that the centreboard will stop pivoting when it is raised. The chock should ideally rest between the bottom of the case and the slot tapes when the board is right down in its gybing position. Raising the board will then stop it gybing — i.e. when beating in strong winds and for downwind work. Mark the head of the board so you know the exact positions needed either to 'fix' the board or to make it gybe.

Centreboard case. Check that the case is parallel throughout its length and depth. In some badly built boats the case is wider in the middle than at its front and back end. If this is so, the leading edge of the centreboard will be tight in the box, with the trailing edge loose — with the result that the board will gybe the wrong way. Similarly, if the bottom of the case is wider than the top (or vice versa), it will be impossible to prevent the board moving from side to side, and the boat won't point.

Make sure that the case sides are rigid throughout their length. If the case top can move, the board will become less effective. Also if the case sides are soft between top and bottom, the board's bend will continue through to its tip, instead of stopping at the base of the centreboard case.

Your boat points, but goes slowly...

CHECK:

Centreboard

If you are using a gybing centreboard it may be gybing through too many degrees. Try fixing some blocks on its forward edge to reduce the angle it gybes through.

Check that the board is the same thickness as used on the top boats. Thicker boards give more lift but more drag; you may be able to get away with a thinner section.

Make sure the leading edge of the foil isn't too round. Again, a sharper edge will be faster, but will stall sooner.

Try raking the board further aft to reduce weather helm and increase speed.

Slot gaskets

Turn the boat over and check the slot gaskets. The best ones I have come across are made from sailcloth with a heavy Mylar core. Fit them by stretching the folded cloth along the bottom of the case and then slide the Mylar between the two layers of sailcloth. Make sure that you have a rubber gasket at the forward edge of the box, which will blend in with the leading edge of the centreboard in its upwind position. The after edge of the slot tapes should be cut away to a vee'd profile so that the water in the case can escape. If the slot tapes are working correctly you will hear the case 'sucking' as the water drains out of the back.

Transom

Make sure that the corner of the transom is built with as sharp an angle as possible. Any round on the edge increases drag where the water leaves the boat.

Rudder

If your class has no limit on the size of rudder and you have never had any steering problems you could well be using too large a blade. Any reduction in size will reduce drag and increase speed. As a rule, go for more depth than width, and keep on reducing the area until you experience a loss of control. You will then know how small an area you can safely get away with.

Sails

In your attempt to increase power and pointing ability you may have set up your sails too full and with the leech too tight. You must, therefore, 'back track' and go through each setting to try to get the air moving off the sail sooner, so that speed can be increased.

Sheets. Ease both main and jib sheets to increase the twist in both sails. If pointing suffers, bring the boom up to the centreline and move the jib fairleads inboard whilst maintaining the same sheet tension.

continued

Sails *continued*	*Depth of camber*. If easing the sheets does not work then your sails must be set with excessive camber, and you must increase mast bend and open up the slot. Move the jib fairleads aft and increase sheet tension to keep the telltales breaking together. Look up the mainsail, and if the top telltale is breaking before there is any sign of horizontal creases forming out of the luff, then angle the spreaders aft. The top telltale should just break before the sail inverts. Add or remove chocks to keep the mast bend even from deck to tip, and remember that rig tension will be reduced when bend is increased. Therefore, increase tension to maintain the current sag in the luff of the jib. *Position of camber*. Increase the tension on both mainsail and jib cunninghams to pull the flow forward and increase twist. *Outhaul*. Pull the outhaul all the way out to the black band to flatten and open up the leech of the mainsail. *Vang*. Transfer from using mainsheet to vang tension sooner. Doing this will reduce power and pointing may suffer. The gain in speed, however, may more than compensate for this, and leeway will be reduced because you are going faster. *Battens*. Try using a stiffer top batten to flatten and twist open the head of the sail sooner. *Rake*. Move the heel of the mast forward. This rakes the mast aft and increases the distance between the mainsail and the jib.
Mast	*Side bend*. Give the helm to your crew and sight up the mast. Check that the middle of the spar is not bending to leeward. If it is, the slot width will be reduced and speed will be poor. This can happen when the spreaders are very long combined with slack rigging tension. The weather shroud will be under more tension than the leeward one, forcing the middle of the mast down via the spreaders. To solve the problem, increase the rig tension; if that doesn't work, shorten the spreaders. If speed is still poor it may be necessary to increase the width of the slot still further. You could try moving the jib fairleads aft (to increase twist) or outboard, though both will reduce pointing ability. The other solution is to move the mast away from the jib. You can achieve this either by letting the spar bend sideways via the spreaders' deflections, or by leaving the mast 'floating' in the mast gate. The latter is preferable as the side bend can be controlled according to wind strength. Removing chocks from the side of the gate will increase bend because the boom forces the mast up to weather, and the slot will become wider. Note that 1/4 inch (6 mm) of movement at deck level will result in inches of bend higher up the spar.

Mast *continued*	*Mast weight*. In flat water the total weight of the mast is not too important. Although a heavy mast will increase all-up weight and heel, it will not make significant speed differences in these conditions. In waves, however, mast weight becomes more critical. Every time the boat goes over and down a wave, the tip of the spar moves approximately twice the distance the bow does. So if your bow lifts, say, 2 feet, the mast swings through 4 feet. Having stepped your mast in the dinghy park, you know how difficult it is to hold it up when it is leaning at such an angle. When sailing it is your boat that does the same job, and the result is a huge increase in pitching motion. Pitching slows the boat by digging the bow and stern deeper into the water and disturbing the air's flow over the sails. A saving, therefore, of one or two pounds (say a kilogram) will be very significant, especially if the weight is taken out of the upper half of the mast. *Tip bend*. Checking the centre of gravity of the mast will give you an idea of the stiffness of your topmast (i.e. the section above the hounds). Although desirable for boats that are over-canvassed or for heavy crews, a stiff top-mast may not be suitable for your boat as power will not be released through the head of the mainsail so quickly. Letting the mast bend off sideways increases the twist in the sail and flattens the camber around the top batten area. Some masts are specifically designed for this purpose, with the top section of the spar flicking open in gusts or when the wind rises above a certain strength. This type of mast may suit you if you are light or if you are having problems with speed in a straight line rather than with pointing angle.

Your boat has no speed on a broad reach ...

CHECK: **Mainsail**	*Mast bend*. Have you more mast bend than the leaders? If so, your mainsail will be flatter and less powerful than theirs. Cure the problem either by increasing the number of chocks, or by decreasing either shroud tension or jib halyard tension. *Foot camber*. Is your mainsail as full in its base when the outhaul is eased as your competitors? Most mainsails are constructed incorporating a 'lens foot' design. When eased, the lower half <div align="right">*continued*</div>

Mainsail *continued*	of the sail transforms from being very flat to being extremely full, creating more power and speed. *Leech twist*. Have a photo taken of your boat from the leeward side to check on mainsail leech twist, and compare it with faster boats (leech twist is discussed in chapter 3).
Jib	*Sheet*. Make sure the sail is well eased so that the windward telltales are just lifting. *Cunningham*. Ease the cunningham right off. *Fairleads*. Check that your fairleads are as far outboard as the faster boats.
Centreboard & case	*Rake*. Try raising the board more to see if speed increases. *Heel*. Heel the boat to windward or leeward until the helm is neutral. *Slot tapes*. Look down into the case and check that the water is escaping out of the back and not rising up the sides. If there is more than two inches (50 mm) of water your slot tapes are not working correctly. *Tip section*. Have a look at the tip of your centreboard. When raised for offwind work the tip of the board begins to work in a different way. It should be faired into either a point or a shallow V. A round section is usually slow and should be avoided.
Rudder	Is there any vibration in the rudder? If so, it will be creating drag. *Cavitation*. Check that both sides of the blade are the same. If not, cavitation will occur as the water flows over each side at a different speed. *Leading edge*. Check that the leading edge is symmetrical. *Fairness*. Run a straight edge over the blade's surfaces and eliminate any bumps or hollows. *Rudder stock*. Have a look over the transom to check that the rudder stock is clear of the water. Any 'spouts' or disturbances are causing drag, and the problem should be cured by raising the entire assembly higher up the transom.
Bailers	Try closing the bailers to see if speed increases. I always fit just one mini bailer, and then use transom flaps to clear the bulk of the water. Only use the bailers when you have water to clear. If they are down at other times they are causing drag.
Spinnaker	*Design*. Check that the sail is the same make and design as used on the faster boats.

Spinnaker ***continued***	*Condition.* Check its age. If it is too old it may have stretched out of shape. *Leech tapes.* Take a look at the tapes on both leeches. If they are made from cheap material they may have shrunk; if so the air will not be leaving the sail cleanly, and you will also have to oversheet to prevent the luff from breaking. If the tapes have been put on too slackly the sail will be too straight in its entry, giving you no warning of when it's going to collapse; you will then be forced to oversheet. *Leech lengths.* Check that both leeches are the same length. Bad seaming or more use on one gybe than the other can both affect the leech lengths. *Guy.* Be sure that the guy is cleated so that the pole is not resting against the forestay. If it is, the load will be transferred from a forward pull to a side thrust. *Trim.* Make sure you're trimming the spinnaker correctly (see chapter 4). Have some photographs taken of your own and faster boats to compare pole height and general spinnaker setting.

You have problems close reaching ...

CHECK:	
Crew weight	Do the boats beating you have heavier crews, or are they carrying more water bottles or weight? On reaches like this there is no substitute for weight, and if you are light you may be doing everything else right and still lose out. So be sure to carry maximum weight in the form of bottles or jackets to boost performance.
Spinnaker	Is your sail as small and as flat as the faster boats? On a tight reach the smaller, flatter kites are always faster. Many Fireball sailors choose extremely small spinnakers just for the first two reaches of the 60 degrees championship course. Providing there is a strong breeze they always gain more on the reaches than they lose on the run.

continued

Vang	Ease the vang right off. This drops air out of the mainsail leech and also raises the boom, which in turn allows the clew of the spinnaker to fly higher. Unless your boat has an extremely high boom, the spinnaker sheet will be held down on a tight reach by the boom. So your vang not only controls the mainsail's leech tension, but also the spinnaker's.
Other controls	Check that you have maximum cunningham and outhaul, and that your jib is not oversheeted.

Your boat has no speed on the run ...

CHECK:	
Mast rake	Check that you have no more aft mast rake than the leaders.
Spinnaker	*Size*. See if the faster boats are using bigger spinnakers. *Pole*. Check the pole height and angle. *Condition*. If the wind is light, make sure the spinnaker is dry.
Centreboard	Raise the centreboard further up.
Rudder	Lift the rudder 10 degrees and feel if you have lee or weather helm. If you have either, correct by heeling the boat.

POINTING
1 A closed leech gives good pointing ability.
2 An open leech gives good speed but reduces pointing ability.
    The same is true of the jib leech: open (3) for speed or closed (4) for pointing.

1

2

3

4

POINTING

Above: mast bend to weather. In strong winds this may be useful because it opens the slot and reduces power. In light winds the mast *must* be straight sideways.

Right: outhaul on (1), and off (2). Note that in (2) the mainsheet has had to be eased to keep the top telltale flowing.

1

2

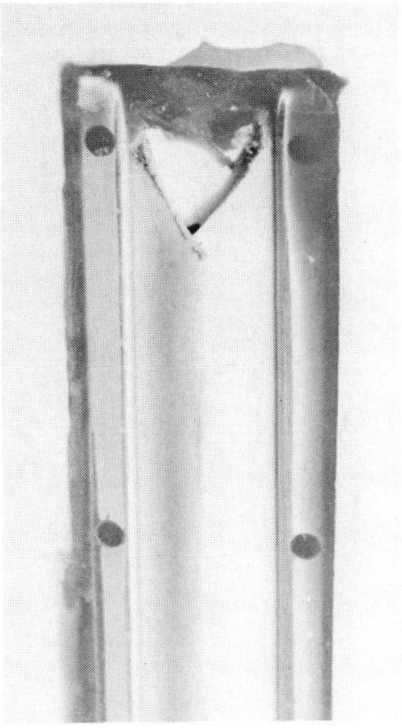

1

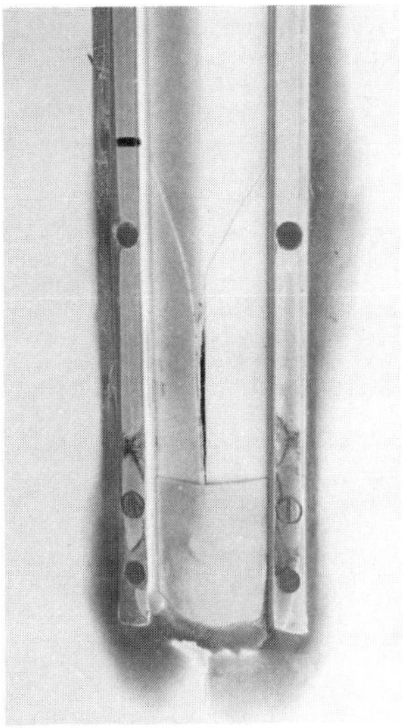

2

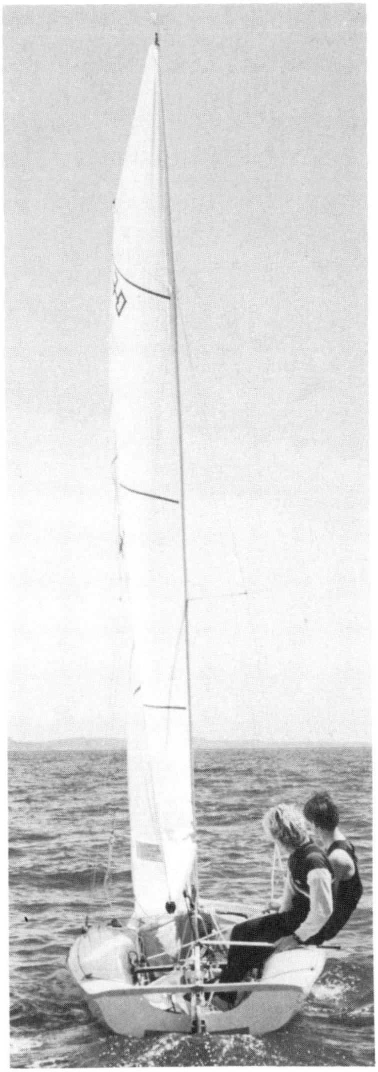

3

POOR SPEED

1 Centreboard gaskets: back of centreboard case. Note the cut-out to allow water to escape from the case.
2 Front of centreboard case; the rubber seal takes up the shape of the leading edge of the board when beating.
3 Increase twist (and boatspeed) by easing sheets, pulling on the cunningham or tightening the outhaul.

1

2

3

REACHING

Lens foot closed (1) and open (2) for reaching.
3 Keep the rudder stock clear of the water.

RUN
Heel the boat until your helm is neutral (lift from the rudder does no good on a run).

Other books in the Sail to Win series

Tactics   *Rodney Pattisson*
A guide to boat-to-boat tactics and strategy around an Olympic course, by gold medallist Rodney Pattisson.

Dinghy Helming   *Lawrie Smith*
One of Britain's top helmsmen gives specific advice on maximising boatspeed in all conditions, plus helming skills required during the race itself.

Dinghy Crewing   *Julian Brooke-Houghton*
Crewing a modern racing dinghy is a complex and demanding task. Olympic medallist Julian Brooke-Houghton explains the skills required and shows how helmsman and crew work together as a race-winning team.

Wind Strategy   *David Houghton*
Most 'sailing weather' books are too large-scale to be relevant to racing on inland or coastal waters. This book shows how to predict the wind over the racecourse area, during the time-span of the race, using simple 'rules of thumb'.

The Rules in Practice   *Bryan Willis*
It is a popular fallacy among racing sailors that you need to know the rules. You *do* need to know your rights and obligations on the water — the rules can always be looked up afterwards. International rules expert Bryan Willis looks at the key situations that repeatedly occur on championship courses, from the viewpoint of each helmsman in turn, and summarises what you may, must or cannot do.

Also published by Fernhurst Books

Sailing the Mirror   *Roy Partridge*
Topper Sailing   *John Caig*
The Laser Book   *Tim Davison*
Laser Racing   *Ed Baird*
Yacht Crewing   *Malcolm McKeag*
Yacht Skipper   *Robin Aisher*
Boardsailing: a beginner's manual   *John Heath*
Board Racing   *Geoff Turner & Tim Davison*
Dee Caldwell's Book of Freestyle Boardsailing   *Dee Caldwell*
Must I go down to the sea again?   *Lesley Black/illustrated by Mike Peyton*
Knots & Splices   *Jeff Toghill*